AFFILIATE MARKETING

Proven Step by Step Guide to Make Passive Income with Affiliate Marketing

Mark Smith

Table of Contents

Introduction

I want to thank you and congratulate you for purchasing the book, *"Affiliate Marketing – Proven Step By Step Guide to Make Passive Income with Affiliate Marketing"*.

This book contains proven steps and strategies on how to start off on the extremely exciting and successful journey of Affiliate Marketing Programs. This book gives you a fairly detailed perspective on what is affiliate marketing, how does it work, what is the common lingo you need to learn and master, the importance of creating and maintaining a great blog and/or website, and the top well-established affiliate partners you should definitely sign up with.

I have also dedicated one chapter on the different ways you can leverage your presence and popularity in the social media to back your affiliate programs. Unfortunately, like all things in the world, affiliate programs are also home to a few scamsters and hoodwinkers ready to pounce upon innocent victims and deprive them of money and other valuables. This book has a chapter on how to identify and avoid such dishonest business entities and people.

What is Affiliate Marketing?

The Internet, or the World Wide Web, began its grand growth phase during the 1990s and since then, there has been no looking back for the amazing and ever-expanding technological element. As with the advent of anything new, companies are also looking out for ways to leverage it for marketing. And the Internet was one big unlimited advertising and marketing space for companies small, big, or medium.

Consumers were being serviced in every nook and corner of the world and suddenly for a lot of organizations the size of their target audience grew multifold and continues to grow as more and more people are getting on to the internet especially so in large emerging economies.

The emergence of search engines has added to the power of the Internet and has given rise to a gigantic platform that can support both information and e-commerce. Owners of websites are leveraging on great content to enhance traffic and business owners are riding piggyback on the websites and blogs to enhance their own customer reach and base.

Affiliate marketing is based on relationships and ideally includes three primary stakeholders: the advertiser, the publisher, and the consumer. Let me give you a brief on each of these stakeholders:

Advertiser- In affiliate marketing, an advertiser is anyone who wants to sell his or her products. The advertiser category includes companies looking to sell their products too. The products being sold can range from electronic goods to food items to air tickets to insurance and investment products and more. The critical element here is as an advertiser you must be willing to pay people who help in promoting and selling your product(s) and business.

Publisher- A publisher could be a company or an individual who promotes and sells the advertiser's products and business in lieu of a charge or commission. The advertiser and the publisher enter into a contract wherein the former will provide marketing online materials such as online advertising banners, website links, and text ads which the latter will incorporate into his or her website.

Consumer- The final and the most important party in the triangular affiliate marketing setup is the consumer. The consumer is the one who sees the advertisement and takes action which could include clicking on a link directed to the advertiser's website or filling up a form that the advertiser has requested for. This completion of action by the consumer is called conversion, which is what is tracked for commission payments due to the publisher.

A Brief History of Affiliate Marketing

Affiliate marketing works such that advertisers reward publishers for every new consumer and/or new business transaction that publishers bring in through their own marketing efforts.

The era before the Internet- Although the phrase "Affiliate Marketing" is conventionally an online term, the affiliate concept existed even before the advent of the Internet. For that matter, the concept still exists in an offline mode. A classic example is when your beautician or hairdresser gives you a discount if you refer a friend to her or him.

A huge difference between offline and online mode is that in the offline of old-world brick-and-motor mode, the reach of affiliate marketing is nowhere as wide as that of the Internet mode. Another key difference between the offline and online affiliate marketing programs is that of tracking your referrals. In the online mode, this has been automated and works like a charm and there is not a single converted lead that gets missed out whereas in the offline mode, tracking and getting paid for referrals is quite a logistical nightmare.

The Internet revolution- The Internet is, perhaps, the most profound discovery of the 20th century. It has changed the way we lead our lives. The Internet has influenced every aspect of our lives including advertising. Consumers have started looking for information, opinions, product reviews, and other details on the Internet and hence it has become a powerful tool in the hands of advertisers.

As technology advanced and newer versions of the Internet were released, the effect of advertising could be tracked more easily. With the introduction of cookies in Web 2.0, you could easily check the effect of your advertising campaigns on your purchase funnel. And moreover, the enhanced levels of blogging by consumers, the huge amount of content that is being generated on the web and the opening up of the e-commerce platform was a perfect stage for the onset of affiliate marketing.

The concept of affiliate marketing as is popular today was designed, patented, and implemented for use by William J Tobin. The first affiliate program was set up by W J Tobin for his company, P C Flowers and Gifts. Amazon then launched its affiliate project called Associates Program in 1996 that is considered as an important milestone in the world of affiliate marketing. Amazon's Associate Program garnered far-reaching global interest and many retailers used it as a model to form their own affiliate programs.

Clickbank and Commission Junction opened their affiliate networks in 1998 and with the advent of these networks, affiliate marketing became far more accessible than before especially for smaller retailers. These two networks facilitated exchanges between affiliates and merchants and also offered payment solutions. In 2000, the United States Federal Trade Commission released a set of norms and guidelines for affiliate marketing that gave the online marketing realm a seal of government approval. In 2008, various legislations in the form of new disclosure guidelines and the Affiliate Nexus Tax helped in the streamlining and regulation the field of affiliate marketing.

With the above short history and a basic understanding of "what is affiliate marketing", I would like to reiterate the power of this advertising tool to help you improve your own financial status by connecting you to millions of internet viewers all across the world including bustling, highly populous and cosmopolitan cities like New York, Singapore, London, LA, Beijing, Tokyo and more to the really remote areas of emerging economies like India, Brazil, and the interiors of China.

I hope this book gives you the required charge to help you take off and sustain a highly profitable affiliate marketing program through your social media pages and/or your own blog and website.

Chapter 1: How Does Affiliate Marketing Work?

Affiliate marketing leverages on "cookies," an innocuous and simple technology which was integrated into Web 2.0, to target a specific audience and hence increase the chances of lead conversions greatly. A cookie also helps in identifying, tracking, and avoiding spam and malware and also helps in enhancing the effectiveness of affiliate marketing.

What is a cookie?

A cookie is a technology that collaborates with web browsers to track and store critical marketing data such as user registration and login information, shopping cart contents, and user preferences. I am sure there are numerous times when you have clicked on "Yes" for the computer question, "Do you want your user id and password remembered for this website?" That is an example of a cookie.

Do you notice that when you browsing the web for something, you find a lot of travel based ads and deals coming up on the side? This is because you have been "cookied," that is to say, when you have searched for travel deals earlier, that search has been stored by the cookies and hence target-based ads are hitting other websites that you are browsing. Cookies are great ways to help advertisers track user preferences and send them display banners and consumer deals that match the user's needs. In such cases, wherein what the advertiser's products are perfect matches for the consumer needs, the chances of lead conversions are high.

Cookies track and record the following kinds of information with respect to consumers:

- Website links you have clicked on

- Website ads you have clicked on

- Websites you have visited

- Time and date when you clicked on any link

- Time and date when you visited websites

- What kind of content and websites you like most

When a consumer visits a publisher's website, liked and clicked on the advertiser's website link and/or ad, the consumer's web browser received the tracking cookie and identifies and stores the following information:

- Who is the advertiser?

- Who is the publisher?

- Which is the ad or link that has been clicked?

- Commission amount due to the publisher

All the above information is stored in the link information under the "parameters" field. This field also contains other anonymous data that is employed for attribution.

What are affiliate networks?

Affiliate networks such as Google Affiliate Network, ClickBank, Commission Junction, and more are hubs that connect publishers and advertisers. These networks have the technological wherewithal to track transactions and leads, offer payment solutions and requisite reports. Advertisers, of course, have the option of using these established networks for their programs or employ their own in-house platform.

Let us take a specific link and learn and understand how some of the critical identifiers are used and stored in the link information, which is then used, by affiliate networks and/or advertisers to track and make payments. The following is an example of a link:

```
<a            href="http://www.tkqlhce.com/click-5377085-
10590299?sid=012-123"                    target="_blank">
webservices.cj.com</a><img       border="0"       height="1"
src="http://www.ftjcfx.com/image-5377085-10590299"
width="1" height="1" border="0" />
```

The following features of the link are critical affiliate marketing-based information that you need to know and be aware of:

Publisher website ID (or PID) - In the above example, the PID is 5377085 which is the unique identification of the publisher. A marketing affiliate program usually gives a publisher one unique ID and under that he, she, or the company could have multiple accounts. For example, you as a publisher could have multiple websites all of which could be linked to this unique PID.

As a publisher, you will be able to promote the advertiser's business, services, and products by the display of ads, banners, text links, search boxes and more. Whenever successful leads for the advertiser are generated from your website, you get paid commissions which are usually a percentage of the actual sale or a fixed amount depending on the sale transaction.

Ad ID (or AID) – In the above example, the AID is 10590299 and identifies the specific link. This AID allows the tracking of the performance of the particular link in question and also allows the publisher to get paid commission. Every link has a unique AID allowing for tracking of advertisers appropriately.

An advertiser is also known as a merchant, brand, or retailer and he or she sells a product or service. Advertisers and publishers partner with each other in an effort to increase sales. Advertisers are happier with affiliate programs than other forms of advertisements, as under this scheme they need to shell out commission amounts only on converted leads.

Shopper ID (or SID) - This identification helps the publisher track his or her referred action generators. This data is then used to reward and target shoppers. The visitor's details are recorded whenever he or she makes a purchase and/or completes a lead form. The transaction made is also tracked and stored for reference. Advertisers and publishers depend on shoppers to make a success of their commercial venture.

Working details of an affiliate marketing program

- The various steps and processes that are part of an affiliate program are given below for your easy reference:

- As an affiliate, you first sign up with the advertiser either through an affiliate network or directly. After the contract is signed, you will get a special affiliate URL or link containing the affiliate's username/ID.

- You then use this link for display on your website. Sometimes, the advertiser could send you creative content or banners to appear on your website. These details usually form part of the agreement.

- When a visitor to your website clicks on the advertiser's

12

link, a cookie from the advertiser is dropped onto the visitor's computer.

- The customer then makes a purchase or does a required transaction on the advertiser's link.

- When the visitor completes the transaction, the advertiser will check the cookie on the computer and find your affiliate ID and give you credit for the transaction.

- The advertiser then updates all relevant reports that reflect visitor traffic as well as sales that your affiliate link has generated.

- Commission payments are made on a regular basis, normally monthly, based on the sales and/or leads generated. These are clearly spelt out in the agreement contract signed by the advertiser and publisher.

Now, that you know and understand what is affiliate marketing and how the processes work, the next chapter deals with commonly used lingo in the affiliate marketing world. This will help you know exactly what your contract terms are and how and when the payments are made.

Benefits of Affiliate Marketing

Affiliate Marketing has become so important in the last few years that in many industries it has predominantly replaced offline marketing. In affiliate marketing, you do not need to invest any time and effort in creating a product or service to sell. Once you have a platform to sell a product or service, you can start selling those products or services.

Companies and individuals can utilize the power of affiliate marketing to earn profit from each sale they are making. Other than these, here are the other benefits of affiliate marketing:

Outsourcing

Most affiliates are experts when it comes to search engine marketing, which will provide you with the chance of getting to the top of search engines like Google or Yahoo without the need to spend too much money on Search Engine Optimization.

Affiliate marketing is one of the fastest ways for small companies to be exposed to the market since advertisements can be placed on various websites. Businesses can also save time in affiliate marketing since there is no need to search and find potential customers anymore.

No Fixed Hours

When you start affiliate marketing, you are also the one setting up your own working hours. When you work for a boss, you work when they tell you. There might also be times when they will ask you to work after your working hours just to have a job done.

Working at your own time means you can choose the ideal time when you think your body will be at the peak of its concentration. If your peak time is from 6 in the morning until 10 in the morning, then you can work during those hours. You may just choose to resume your work again in the afternoon, during peak hours again. If you are working for a boss with a dictated timeframe, you cannot choose to work with your body, which may affect your work nonetheless.

Only Incur Fixed Costs

There is no budget wasted when it comes to affiliate marketing. The amount paid to the affiliates is the cost of sale. The business owner will set the bounty and they will only pay when sales are made.

Find-ability

Once a consumer visits search engines like Google and Yahoo, multiple listings will be directed and linked to the business, which will provide a better chance of being found compared to the other competitors who only have one to two links on the first page.

Visibility

High search engine listings can be secured by the affiliates and they can display advertisements on their websites. In referring customers, an affiliate only needs a website. This is free brand, product or service exposure that does not have any down time.

Better prospects and acquisitions

The affiliates can choose the ads they wish to use and advertise on their websites. These affiliates know who their audiences and future clients are. Because of this, they can pick the campaigns most suited to attract these prospects to their demographic. It is based on the affiliate's interests to pick the ads that the audience will mostly likely respond to.

Cost Effective

Affiliate Marketing is the most cost-effective when it comes to direct marketing options. Other direct marketing options like multimedia, billboards and pay-per-click advertising may be

15

effective but are also expensive. There is no budget wasted when it comes to affiliate marketing since no payment is needed to be given to an affiliate unless a visitor becomes a customer.

Chapter 2: Commonly Used Lingo in Affiliate Marketing

Before venturing out on anything new, learning the basic communication skills is critical to making a success of the venture. How the various aspects of a new business are named, what the names mean, what words do the various stakeholders use to communicate with each other, code language used; all these elements are extremely important to learn and master before you plunge into a new business AD-VENTURE.

Being familiar with terms that are used in the business helps you gain confidence when you are speaking to people associated with the business. This improved confidence aids in improving the success of your venture. Using the same lingo puts you on par with the experienced in the field and enhances your confidence level significantly.

This chapter is dedicated to helping you learn the commonly used terms and lingo in affiliate marketing. I have arranged the words and phrases alphabetically to facilitate an easy search. So here goes:

Above the fold – This is that part of the website or blog which a visitor views without scrolling down. This part is the first thing to be made visible when the page loads.

Adware – Many times referred to as spyware, this is usually part of free software in which unnecessary and annoying advertisements are included. Moreover, many times, these software programs are difficult to uninstall and can create a lot of nuisance for consumers. Established advertisers normally do not want to associate themselves with affiliates who use this rather deceitful method of advertising.

Affiliate Agreement – This is a contract sent to you whenever you initiate a new relationship with a merchant and/or affiliate network. It is a legally binding document that contains rules, regulations, responsibilities, expectations, and other critical legalities concerning both sides of the affiliate partnership namely the publisher and the advertiser. It is the terms of service between the two parties, which oversees and defines the affiliate relationship.

Affiliate Link – This is the unique link provided to you at the start of the relationship by the advertiser. This unique link identifies you as the affiliate whenever traffic from your blog and/or website is being directed to the advertiser's website. This link helps to track the sales and traffic generated by your marketing efforts. The affiliate special link or URL is embedded with the affiliate's username and/or ID.

Affiliate Managers – Affiliate managers are people who help advertisers manage their affiliate programs. These people carry the onus to recruit affiliates, ensure affiliates are promoting their products and services in a legitimate manner, and to increase sales from affiliates. Affiliate managers are usually a bridge between the affiliate and the advertiser. They could either be in-house employees of the advertiser or offer services as third party vendor such as affiliate networks.

Affiliate Network – Affiliate networks are third-party service providers that help advertisers manage their affiliate marketing programs. These networks help connect the advertiser and the affiliates thereby enhancing the advertiser's reach. They also offer the required back-end technological support to keep track of and record and deliver reports regarding traffic and sales generation leads created by the publisher. They also ensure that the publisher is paid correctly and as per the signed contract.

Affiliate networks facilitate the enhancement of available programs both for the advertiser and the publisher on a common platform. Some very popular affiliate networks that operate in the market today are Commission Junction, Amazon Associates, and ClickBank.

Affiliate Program – An affiliate program is one that is offered by advertisers to publishers wherein the latter refers people to the products and services of the former. The advertiser pays a predetermined commission to the publisher in return for the said referrals. Affiliate programs are also referred to as partner, associate, revenue, or referral-sharing program. Many advertisers use their **in-house** affiliate programs that are referred to as **indie programs** the full form of which is "independent affiliate programs."

Approval – Merchants or advertisers give either manual or auto approval to partner with affiliates. **Manual approval** entails the advertiser to look at each application individual and give his or her approval for the affiliate's participation in the program. **Auto approval** means that the advertiser approves all affiliate applications instantly and automatically.

Banner Ad – Banner ads are visual graphical ads of the merchants that are displayed on the publisher's website.

Charge Back – There could be times when a customer referred by you buys the advertiser's products and/or services but cancels the order later on. During the interim, the advertiser may have paid your commission. On cancellation of his order, the advertiser will deduct the amount of the commission paid to you and this deduction is called charge back.

In those affiliate programs which pay for lead generation, this charge back can be triggered if the advertiser feels that the referrals are fraudulent.

Cloaking – Cloaking is obscuring content from a webpage or it could also entail hiding affiliate tracking codes within links. Content hiding is against prescribed norms whereas hiding tracking codes is allowed and is commonly practiced in the field of affiliate marketing for increased click counts and other marketing advantages.

Click Fraud – There are many affiliate programs that pay based on pay-per-click. In an attempt to get paid more, there are many people who merely click on the said link without having any real interest in the advertiser's products and services. These fraudulent clicks never get converted into sales and hence are referred to as click frauds.

Commission – This is the amount of money received by the affiliate from the advertiser for providing referrals and/or sales leads. This amount is usually a predefined element that is paid if the desired outcome is realized by the advertiser owing to the marketing efforts of the affiliate. Commissions are sometimes referred to as **customer bounty** too.

Contextual link – This is a link that is embedded within the content of your blog or website as against being put in the sidebar which is a more conventional form.

Conversion – A conversion is said to be achieved if a visitor to your website has clicked on the advertiser's link and has completed the required action plan such as signing up for the advertiser's website or purchasing a product. Conversions are dependent on the desired result and will vary from advertiser to advertiser. This element is usually included in the affiliate agreement.

Cookies – Though this term is not exclusive to affiliate marketing, the advantage of cookie technology is leveraged by affiliate marketing programs to track and record sales and transactions triggered from the publisher's domain. Cookies are used to assign unique IDs to various users to keep track of conversions and payments.

An example of how a cookie works is given here. Suppose you had written a book review on your website along with a link to buy the product from Amazon. A visitor views the book reviews and clicks on the link to buy the book. However, for some reason, he or she was not able to complete the transaction. After a couple of days, the visitor goes directly to Amazon and buys the book. Since the cookie had already been inserted by Amazon into the visitor's computer when he or she clicked the affiliate link from your website, you will get the commission for this purchase as the sale is attributed to you despite the fact that the visitor bought the book later on and without coming to your website again.

Cookie Retention/Expiration – Every cookie comes with an expiry date after which the cookie gets dropped from the customer's computer. If the customer chooses to complete the purchase after the cookie is expired, the sale is not attributed to you. Usually, the cookie is retained for 30-90 days; however, there are some wherein the duration of retention is much shorter.

Cookie Stuffing – This is a sneaky way to get more sales attributions by unscrupulous affiliates. Cookies are deliberately and sneakily inserted from the advertiser's website to the consumer's computer without the user actually visiting the affiliate's website. This method is done based on the fact that someday the consumer would visit the advertiser's site and make the purchase that would then be attributed to the affiliate who had sneaked in the cookie.

This kind of underhand dealing is frowned upon by all legitimate users and these kinds of affiliates are also banned from many programs. So, it is important to know such underhand dealings do exist and there are ways and means to catch and ban the culprit. Never ever indulge in this method of unscrupulous affiliate marketing!

CPA – The full form of CPA is Cost Per Acquisition/Action. This is what the advertiser pays the publisher based on the qualifying action taken by consumers that are directed from the publisher's website. Commonly used actions include sign-ups and completed sales.

CPA is sometimes referred to as CPO (Cost Per Order) or CPS (Cost Per Sale) and refers to the amount paid by the advertiser to the publisher for every qualifying order or sale.

CPC – The full form of CPC is cost per click and as the name suggests, refers to the payment made by the advertiser for every click on his or her online ad that is displayed on the publisher's website.

CPL – The full form of CPL is cost per lead and again as the name suggests, it is the amount paid by the advertiser to the publisher for every qualified lead which could be in the form of email ID, completed registration forms, a survey form, or any other as described in the affiliate agreement.

CTR – The full form of CTR is Click-Through Ratio/Rate that is a metric normally employed in direct selling advertising. This ratio represents the percentage of visitors to the affiliate's site who have clicked on the advertiser's link.

Datafeed – Datafeed is a file containing all product details of a particular advertiser. The details include descriptions, images, and prices of the products along with your affiliate link. Datafeed is highly useful when you are establishing an online store that features affiliate products.

Disclosure – A notice or page on your website telling your visitors that you are being paid or compensated for buying products, service endorsements, and recommendations made by you is called disclosure. This is in accordance with Federal Trade Commission laws.

EPC – The full form of EPC is Earnings Per Click that is the average income you earn as an affiliate for every click. To calculate EPC, you would need to divide the amount of commission earned by the total number of clicks on the affiliate link. Here is an example to illustrate EPC: suppose you have earned $4000 as earnings in the entire lifetime of your affiliate membership for a particular link and the total number of clicks is 12,000, then the EPC would be 4000/12000 = 33 cents.

First Click – This is one way in, which an affiliate program works. Let me explain this term with an example. Let us assume that a visitor came to your site and clicked on the advertiser's link but did not make the purchase that time. After some days, suppose this visitor went to another affiliate's site, clicked on the same advertiser's link and makes the purchase.

This advertiser attributes this sale to you because the first click to the advertiser's website was from your link. However, this transaction must happen within the cookie expiry date. To reiterate, since the first click to the merchant site was from your site, you are given attribution for the sale providing it is completed before cookie expiry date.

Last Click Attribution – This is another way an affiliate program works. This is the opposite of first click is last click attribution. Whichever site the consumer last visited and clicked on the advertiser's website is given the attribution for the sale, if any. In this case, the earlier clicks are ignored and only the affiliate site from the last click happens is taken into consideration.

Impression – Impressions measure the number of times an ad is displayed on a page. Each time an ad is displayed is equal to one impression.

Master Affiliate Network – Using a JavaScript code that is appropriately placed on your site allows you to link to some or all merchant affiliate programs through a master affiliate network. SkimLinks and VigLink are examples of popular and established master affiliate networks.

Niche – A website that deals with a specific vertical or topic is called a niche site. For example, if your blog is dedicated to cookery, then it would be designated a niche website.

Payment Threshold – Many advertisers require affiliates to accrue a minimum amount threshold to make the commission payment. This limit is called the payment threshold.

PPC – The full form of PPC is pay per click and this payment model entails that the advertiser should make commission payments for every click on the affiliate's advert. Also referred to as cost per click or CPC, this payment model is used by many established advertisers and affiliate networks.

ROAS – The full form of ROAS is Return on Advertising Spend and it is a term used to calculate the revenue received for every dollar expended on advertisements. It is a ratio got by dividing the generated revenue by the cost of advertising and campaigns.

ROI – The full form of ROI is Return on Investment. In simple terms, this is calculated by evaluating the profit (or loss) made against the amount of money invested in the business. The invested amount would be a sum of amounts used for setting up the business, advertising costs, running costs, and more.

PPS and PPL – Pay per sale and pay per lead are commonly used payment methods in the affiliate marketing field.

Privacy Policy – A page on your website should be dedicated to letting visitors know how you will deal with the private information that they will be giving you via contact forms or through hidden tracking methods. This disclosure norm is a prerequisite to participate in many advertisers' affiliate programs. It is also needed to partner with Google Analytics and Google Adsense

Super Affiliates – The highest earners in any affiliate program are known as the Super Affiliates and normally these people contribute up to 80% of total sales generated by the program. Most advertisers love to partner with super affiliates as this frees up their time to focus on their core competencies as the affiliate marketing tactics are anyway working wonders.

Super Affiliates normally enjoy the power of **co-branding** offered by the merchants wherein the link from the affiliate takes the visitor to the landing page of the advertiser, which contains the brands of both the affiliate and the merchant.

Tracking Code – The tracking is the unique ID given to you by the advertiser when you first sign up the affiliate agreement. This tracking code helps keep track of traffic, sales, and leads generated by you as an affiliate based on which commission payments are made.

White Label – There are some advertisers who allow their products and/or services to be sold by the publisher under his or her own brand. The consumer gets the impression that the product actually belongs to the publisher. This is referred to as white labeling.

Now, that the common and a few uncommon terms are clearly explained to you, the next chapter specifically deals with how important it is to have a great website or blog so that you can attract more visitors and hence enhance the business and marketing opportunities through your blog.

Chapter 3: Blog/Website – A Key Element for Affiliate Marketing Success

Starting and maintaining an epic blog or website is perhaps the most important element to take care of if you are looking to make your affiliate marketing venture a success. If you desire to monetize your blog, then simply putting together and updating a few posts and then hoping for the best in not enough at all. You need to put on your thinking cap, work hard, and create an excellent blog that will attract and retain loyal readers and then rake in money and success for you.

Before you set up your blog, you must know what your niche is, what you are going to write on, and where your traffic is going to come from. You will have to sit down and do some serious research and find a profitable niche that you can write about such that you increase traffic to your blog and then monetize it. The following steps will help you start off a great blog:

- Pick a niche

- Register a suitable domain name

- Get a good web hosting plan or

- Install a popular and well-established blogging platform such as WordPress, Jekyll, Tumblr, etc.

- Create Great Blog Content

How to choose a niche that is profitable for you?

This is, I believe, the most important element in creating a blog that will slowly but surely bring in more traffic and hence deliver unlimited business opportunities. Choosing a wrong niche can be the beginning of the end for you in blogging. Despite beautifully written content, a wonderful blog design, and great pictures - if the right niche is not chosen, you will not succeed in monetizing your blog.

There are various ways to find the most profitable niche and here are some of them:

Follow the money trail – Look out for those niches wherein companies are spending the most amount of money towards advertising. This method is the most sensible way to find your profitable niche because companies will not be spending that kind of money unless they are sure Returns on Investment are coming by boatloads.

How do you find a profitable niche using this method? Simple! Use Google Keyword Planner and search for the keywords using a search such as Google or Bing. If there are more than 3 or 4 advertisements coming up on the side for the same keywords, then you can be sure this is a profitable niche to take up.

Google Keyword Planner will again help you find what the average price of a click is for that niche and you will be able to estimate the earnings you can make from Google Adsense.

Another way to find a profitable niche is to leverage information from Spyfu; a fairly accurate search analytics tool. Spyfu gives you the keywords and key phrases that advertisers are paying for and how much. Commission Junction (CJ.com) will also help you find a niche that is profitable.

Facebook – Facebook, other than being the world's biggest social media network, is also a very useful tool to find out if the niche you want to choose has the potential to make you money or not. Create and follow your Facebook Page to know and understand your fans better. Learn about their profiles, their likes and dislikes; use suggestions from Facebook to check out competition etc.

Old-world Keyword Research – Despite the seeming antiquity of this method, believe me, it works really well to decide on a profitable niche. With the right key phrase you can garner a lot of information based on which you can choose to or leave out the niche you are researching:

The level of competition – more the number of searches; higher the demand for the niche

Name of relevant brands and companies

Intentions of the searchers – Invariably people using the widget review are people keen on making the purchase. Phrases such as "widget name and number," "top widget brands," "buy widget online," etc. indicate a better chance of completed sales whereas phrases such as "complain widget," "widget history," etc. have lesser chances of completed sales.

Register a suitable domain name

Here are a few tips to help you choose a good domain name:

- Stick to .com as most searches are done with .com rather than other options such as .net, .tv, .info, etc. The .net option is a good one too, but try and get the .com option

- Keep your domain name short, simple, and sweet

- The domain name should be easy to spell and

remember. Avoid complex and obscure words and phrases.

- Avoid hyphens in your domain name

- Remember to include the keyword in your domain and keeping it at the beginning of the name is better than keeping it at the end. For example, if "flying bats" is the keyword, then a domain name like flyingbatsaregreat.com is better than comeseemyflyingbats.com

- Do not be depressed by the fact that the "perfect" domain name you chose is already taken; come back to the drawing board and start again. Remember perseverance pays.

Get a good web hosting plan – There are many web hosting services companies available in the market. The top established hosting sites with a proven track record include Go Daddy and Blue host. Visit their websites and choose a plan that suits your needs and wallet the best.

Install a popular and well-established blogging platform

There are many people who recommend the use of your own website via a web hosting service instead of using a free blogging platform. As there are advantages and disadvantages for both, you can do research and make suitable choices. Here is a list of some popular free blogging platforms that are used by people all across the world:

WordPress.Com – This free blogging platform (any upgrades come at a cost) is, perhaps, the most popular blogging platform in the world today. WordPress works really well for those not wanting customizations and added plugins. It is a great way to test and strengthen your blogging skills here without having to spend time and money on your own blog.

Tumblr – Again, a free blogging platform, Tumblr is easy to set up. You can start blogging immediately and the "reblog" function of this platform is a great tool.

WordPress.org – The main difference between WordPress.com and WordPress.org is the former is hosted on the server of WordPress whereas the latter is hosted on an external server. There is a small hosting cost for WordPress.org and gives you access to a wide repertoire of themes and plugins that will enhance the profile of your blog immensely!

Create great blog content

Content is king is the oldest and yet the most timeless adage that rings true irrespective of the platform that we use. And nothing is farther from the truth even in making a great commercial success of your blog. Here are a few reasons as to why content was, is, and will continue to be king and why you need to focus on this extremely critical element of your blog:

Great content works wonder for SEO – Original and high-quality content on a website has a large impact on SEO rankings. Regularly published unique content with links to other relevant content along with keywords placed naturally in the text automatically enhances the SEO ranking. A better ranking means more traffic to your blog and hence increased business opportunities too.

Great content enhances visitor engagement – If you write good content, visitors will flock to your website as they will feel more engaged with your writing than with a badly written content. Visitors will be encouraged to leave comments, like, or even share your content thereby enhancing your brand. Another great way to ensure your content to start off well and foster a great consumer relationship is to make sure your content is available on social media too and can be easily shared.

Great content generates sales – When you are content is unique, honest, and transparent, people are more likely to believe what you say and what you display on your pages. This exhorts them to make purchases and click on affiliates' ads on your website thereby leading to increased leads and sales which in turn translate to more money for you. Moreover, the spread of your brand by word of mouth will increase traffic too.

Great content adds value to your readers' lives – Value adding content more often than not is liked by consumers as invariably their daily lives are impacted positively. Educative content such as good, honest product and service reviews, how-to blogs, learning-based videos go a long way in attracting and retaining loyal visitors to your website.

The quality of your blog content has a direct impact on the way you make your earnings through affiliate marketing programs. Do not ever underestimate the power of creating good-quality and unique content. Make sure you update content regularly and thereby increase the chances of making more money via the affiliate marketing route.

Chapter 4: Affiliate Marketing Strategies

Affiliate marketing has undergone tremendous changes since its first appearance in the world of Internet. A lot of regulations and laws have been set up; SEO rankings are fairly ruthless in discarding and punishing thin and low-quality content; there are huge challenges as competition is gaining ground; it is getting really tough to stay ahead in the game of affiliate marketing.

Despite the difficulties, this realm has a lot of opportunities in store and if you work hard and diligently and persist in your endeavors, you are bound to find success. There are many people out there who are making millions through the affiliate marketing channel. There are simple, straightforward, and honest strategies that will help you gain ground here and this chapter lists a few critical and important ones for you:

Stick to a small niche and delve deep

Many first-timers make the common mistake of working with multiple niches and not having the focus to work hard only a couple of them. Instead of creating multiple websites covering many topics, choose 2 or 3 profitable niches and work hard at each of them to increase traffic and garner more sales and leads.

Once you have achieved some amount of success, then you will find the resources to handle more number of niches across various topics. But in the beginning work at a couple and delve really deep instead of only scratching the surface of many niches.

Newcomers to the system often make the mistake of peppering their site or sites with lots of different things, imagining that people are likely to buy more because they have more choice. It is typical human thinking to want a lot of choice in anything and everything, let alone links on a website. But then, this is wrong on so many levels. You are not a store – you don't have to offer your customers choice because they did not land on your site with purchase in mind. They're there for information, and if you're good at what you do, you'll be able to persuade them to buy something while they are there so you can make some cash.

Think of it as a classy gig to have only one website promotion and that website is the best one that your readers can have. That is, you will have the chance to promote one product or service better rather than having to do it for 5 or 6 different ones. Not only will that confuse your customers but it will confuse you as well. You will have to look into two or three different companies and think of where their links will look the best. So in effect, you will be complicating the process for yourself. It is better to have faith in one product or service and promote it to the best of your abilities. Think of yourself as a pop-up store to promote one product as opposed to a supermarket that offers a lot of choices.

Say there is a camping website. In this instance, it would be a good idea to affiliate with a business that retails camping and leisure goods, rather than a single product. Say you write a review article on the latest winter sleeping bags. You can point out the virtues and problems of a product sold by your affiliate, and if you pitch it right, they'll want to buy one. Because they can do it easily from your site, they'll click, and maybe buy something else as well while they're at it.

It is always the power of suggestion that works on a majority of the customers. They will take a liking to something if you tell them that you are offering them the same product that you have personally tested and liked yourself.

On the other hand, if there's too much choice – say you've got links to half a dozen different sleeping bags, as well as the one you've reviewed – they'll go to a price comparison site to check things out. Once they leave your site, it's unlikely they'll return, so you've lost the sale – and the commission. So don't make the mistake of putting up too many choices at once. If you have put up just one and the website is offering it at the best price in the market then even if the person has left your site to do a quick price comparison, he or she is sure to return back to your site to click on the ad.

So, stick with one business or product. If you want to do more, set up a different website for each affiliate, and concentrate on that, rather than spreading yourself too thinly.

Create superior content

A huge challenge that you face as an affiliate is to instill confidence in your visitors and provide value to them. While large companies spend a lot of money creating brands, you have the power to sit down and create such superior content that it would be nearly impossible for search engines not to direct traffic to your site. Spend time and energy to create and update great and engaging content that your visitors will love to read, like, and share. Nothing sells better than word-of-mouth praise from loyal visitors.

Make your site a brand by itself

Many large affiliates in the market started off small and yet with hard work and perseverance, they have been able to create a brand for themselves. This kind of brand building happens with consistent quality content, strong and powerful editorials, and value additions that they offer customers.

Ensure your affiliate programs include recurring revenues

Marketing strategies are extremely fluid in the affiliate realm and what works today need not work tomorrow driven by multiple factors including changes in the ranking algorithm, affiliate programs shutting down, cost cutting in advertising, and more. It is prudent to ensure that some of your revenue is based on recurring revenue even if it means getting paid in smaller amounts but more frequently. While one-time payments are great to increase revenue, they do not offer protection against major changes that could negatively impact your earnings from affiliate programs. It makes sense to slowly build up a recurring revenue foundation within your affiliate program portfolio.

Ensure your visitor traffic is from multiple sources

If you rely only on one source for your traffic, then when that dries up or some drastic changes take place, then your entire affiliate program will come crashing down. So ensure that your content is viewed across multiple platforms thereby enhancing traffic diversification and reducing risk due to the unexpected downfall of a single source.

Make sure your content is good for mobile devices

The usage of mobile devices has grown in leaps and bounds and relying on any technology that does not support these devices is a sure short way to lose out on plenty of business opportunities.

Preempt breakout trends and prepare well for seasonal trends

There are hundreds and thousands of new and emerging breakout trends on the crest of which smart affiliates ride on and make their money before they ebb out. It is critical that you preempt these breakout trends much before and take advantage of them before customers' interests begin to wane. Google Trends is a great way to check for upcoming breakout trends and get ready to cash in on the flood.

Seasonal trends, on the other hand, are easier to predict because they recur regularly and you will know the rise, the peak, and the downward slide well. This will help you prepare for seasonal trends too. These preemptions and preparations will guarantee that you do not lose out on any great opportunity to make a success of your affiliate program.

Participate in affiliate programs that enhance your affiliate income by magnitude

While small value commissions from large traffic inflow are good initially, as you grow and evolve in the affiliate market field, it is important to promote high-value products that will give you increased income per approved lead or sale. Increasing the value of the products you promote is easier than having the increase the traffic inflow multiple times.

Create content that meets changing SEO requirements

As Google is getting more and more sophisticated with its SEO technology and including similar terms to match with keywords, it is important to create content that is in sync with these changing needs. It makes more sense now to have in-text content that is more relevant to readers instead of simply focusing on keywords. Hence, target topics appropriately instead of keywords and phrases.

You must be well versed in the concept of "SEO." SEO refers to search engine optimization. You must have heard that many companies have a good SEO team that helps them to increase their popularity. Well, this is true because these teams work hard in promoting the websites and blogs of the company and help it appear on top of the Google search list.

For this to happen, you need to pick out all the top words from your blog or website, that are most likely going to be typed into search engines by people. If they get the combination of words right then your site is going to appear as the topmost link. For this, you can also make use of a small description that will help you put in all the main words on your site. But remember just a good SEO description will not do the trick and you need to have good content as well.

Promote products that you are very familiar with

Marketing products that you are familiar with has many positives. The first is that you are comfortable talking about its benefits and uses and this confidence comes out in your content. The confidence that is reflected in your writing is invariably felt by the readers and people who want to buy the product will be compelled to do so.

Secondly, there is a sense of satisfaction you will feel that you have been able to convince someone else based on your own experience and hence your feedback is genuine and not misplaced. Such honest marketing strategies will definitely bear fruit sooner than later as the integrity of your recommendations is bound to spread by word of mouth slowly but surely.

Product Review Sites

A classic form of affiliate marketing is to build a product review site that you keep updated regularly with reviews and recommendations of products that you have used. Featuring links to the product's website either on the sidebar or including in the content is a great way to compel customers to buy the product immediately after reading your well-written review. If the review is honest and straightforward your affiliate marketing income will grow by leaps and bounds as you keep adding and updating your site regularly.

Use blogroll or Partner Center

Affiliate links can be placed on a website as a logroll or partner center. The blogroll contains affiliate links to multiple third-party sites that are also blogs. However, these links take visitors to a landing page wherein they can sign up for a product and/or service.

Sites that Aggregate Product Feed

These kinds of sites are also great for affiliate programs. You, as the publisher, would aggregate various kinds of information regarding products and upload it onto your site. The details would usually include images, prices, and specifications of the product. This kind of compelling information and hard facts about the product could drive the customer to click on the link on your site to purchase the product.

Work on your Website First

Affiliate marketing thrives on people's interest in clicking on links to products that catch their eye. But who are these "people"? Well, these are people who will visit your blog or website to read what you have written. So in order to lure these people, you have to make your blog or site as interesting as possible. It is fine to go all out and decorate it as much as you like. But make sure you stick with the intended theme otherwise, people will only visit to mock your blog.

Remember that you need to establish a good reader base in order to land an affiliate marketing gig.

So, it's no good setting up a website today and joining an affiliate marketing program tomorrow. Until you're getting a good number of unique visitors – or impressions - to your website, you're not going to get the click-through to your affiliate. Here, "unique" refers to new customers and not the same old ones who have probably bookmarked you and keep visiting all the time. You must have had several of your friends telling you to check out their blog or site and also who have asked you to visit often and spread the word. Well, they are doing this so that their site or blog has enough "traffic."

Clearly, not everyone is going to click on the links and to get a reasonable amount of clicks, you need plenty of regular visitors. You also need to build up a reputation as an expert in your niche before people will trust you enough to go for your recommendations. It is like running a site that throws up one interesting piece of writing after another in order to lure people into reading it and staying put. That is exactly how your website should operate. There should be interesting content for people to read and remain glued. It is not helpful if they visit just once and immediately forget about your blog.

You need to track the number of people that visit your page and record the numbers per day, per month and per year. This will help you in knowing how popular your blog really is.

So what happens when you have enough visitors? Before you ask, nobody seems to be sure what constitutes 'enough' in this case. Some people say 1,000 impressions a month; others say 1,000 impressions a week. So it is safe to assume that having at least 4000 to 6000 impressions a month will help you in becoming popular enough. Well, then you have to be patient because it will take time to build up revenue. Remember that it is always cumulative and for the number to go high, you need to wait it out. You're not going to be making $ 1,000 dollars while you sleep at the end of the first week. In fact, it could be months or even years before you get to that stage if you ever do. And you certainly won't pull in the big bucks with just one website. Play the patience game, and take the time to learn what works and what doesn't before you dive in with both feet. The more prepared you are, the better the results that will come your way. Putting in a little hard work at the very beginning will help you go a long way in establishing a good line of passive income.

Any or all of these strategies are aimed at increasing traffic to your sites and increasing customer and visitor confidence in your content so that they are driven to clicking on an affiliate link on your site to complete the desired action that translates to affiliate earnings for you. It is important to remember that none of the above-mentioned strategies is a one-format-works-for-all type. You have to factor in what you have chosen to promote and who your target audience is and then make informed choices about the kind(s) of strategies to use.

Notwithstanding the above comment, an honest and upright website that gives correct information and recommendations without exaggeration is key to making a success of your affiliate program ventures. To reiterate, engaging, relevant, and updated content continues to hold sway over all other elements of a great website that attracts and retains loyal visitors.

Chapter 5: Top Affiliate Networks

While it is very difficult to come up with an exhaustive list of affiliate networks and programs for all of you hoping to make a beginning in this highly lucrative realm, this chapter deals with some of the top affiliate networks that have built a great reputation and brand for themselves. You can rest easy that the below-listed networks are above board and are backed by good products that you will be proud to promote on your website.

However, there could be smaller and equally upright networks that work well for you. What works well for you is dependent on many factors including what you plan to promote, who you would like to partner with, what niche is your website, and other such aspects. Please ensure that you have done ample homework on the advertisers and merchants that you choose to partner with before you sign on the dotted line.

Commission Junction – CJ, as it is referred to popularly, is a well-established trusted and consistent affiliate network that is a great company to partner with.

Rakuten Linkshare – This affiliate marketing service provider on advertiser service, large retailers as well as small merchants making its merchant base large enough to fit many affiliates comfortably.

ClickBank – A pioneer this field, ClickBank continues to have the support of smaller merchants and hence is attractive to many affiliates.

Amazon – Another pioneer in the field of affiliate marketing, Amazon has an extremely easy-to-use affiliate interface and has a humongous repertoire of products to choose from. These aspects make Amazon a very popular affiliate network and despite its lower-than-market affiliate payments, it is a great way to have a great head start for you to affiliate with this household name.

AvantLink – A comparatively new player in the market, AvantLink's many strategies are finding a lot of takers, which has made it to one of the top players in the realm of affiliate marketing.

ShareASale – Backed by a perception of integrity and honesty, ShareASale affiliate network has a lot of support from many affiliates across the world.

oneNetwork Direct – A great merchant for software products and services, oneNetwork Direct of Digital River, offers the best in the technological industry and has a presence all across the globe.

RevenueWire – RevenueWire is a specialist in technological products and has built a sterling reputation for ethical and sustainable commerce.

LinkConnector – This fairly large affiliate network offers products from a wide gambit of industries and merchants ranging from the Top 500 retailers on the internet to the smaller niches too.

Pepperjam – With a reputation for being very novice-friendly, Pepperjam affiliate network has a large fan-following both from merchants and super affiliates.

eBay Partner Network – Backed by QCP or Quality Click Pricing methodology for making affiliate payments, eBay Partner Network is a wonderful platform to partner with.

44

Affiliate Window – A hugely popular affiliate network in Britain with a slew of affiliate network awards under its belt, Affiliate Window is now making waves in the US too.

TradeDoubler – A pioneer of affiliate marketing in Europe, TradeDoubler was established in Sweden in 1999. It is still one of the most popular and a great performing affiliate network across all of Europe.

Avangate – Avangate is also an award-winning Europe-based affiliate network and specializes in SaaS and software products

Millionaire Network – Millionaire Network is open to affiliates on an invitation-only basis and focuses primarily on the success of the advertiser.

Zanox – Zanox is another of Europe's large affiliate network with a presence across the continent and an attractive payment scheme that makes it highly popular with affiliates.

WebGains – Backed by some old-fashioned yet robust value-system, this UK-based affiliate network is reputed to have an unshakable ethics-based reputation that is expected to enhance its longevity in the rather nebulous affiliate marketing field.

Adcommunal – This Canada-based affiliate network has grown from strength to strength and is one of the top players on the world stage of affiliate marketing.

PeerFly – A newcomer in the field of affiliate marketing, in a very short time, PeerFly has risen to one of the world's leading network backed by an excellently performing platform and a great team.

Since each site is unique and has its own weaknesses and strengths, it is impossible to come up with a complete list of available affiliate networks. The above list contains only the popular and most commonly used ones. The list highlights some of the large players across the world in the affiliate network realm and a few of them, I am sure, will work for you wonderfully, especially helping you through your steep learning curve.

As you gain more confidence and pick up more skills in the field, you will find more relevant, perhaps, more complex, yet better-paying merchants and advertisers that are in line with your own interests. You could at that time partner with these affiliates too as there are no regulations stopping you from any number of affiliates that you wish to partner with.

Picking the Right Affiliate Program

Now that we've gone into the list of reputed affiliate networks it's important to know how to choose an affiliate program that's good for you. All affiliate programs are different and you need to thoroughly inspect each one before you decide to jump into a deal. This section will cover the various things that you need to keep in my mind when you're finding the program that's the right fit for you.

Terms and Conditions

If you have decided on which company will be best for you and your customers, it's time to talk about terms. After all, that's what it's all about. The first thing to ask is how the program works. Are you paid purely for sales, or do you get a commission for leads? It is always better to argue for the latter as you will be tying up with someone who is considering you for your popularity. So it is best that you make full use of the opportunity and argue in your favor. It can make a big difference when it comes down to dollars, both in the amount you can expect to earn, and how long you will have to get paid.

How often do you get paid, and what is the minimum payout level? Many companies pay at the beginning or end of the month, or they may pay out twice a month – usually on the 15th and last day of the month. If you have a certain preference then you can consider asking them to change the time of payout. Check that the minimum payment threshold is not set too high. Obviously, it's not cost effective to pay out every time somebody clears $10, but if you have to rack up $100 or more before you see the color of your commission, it can be very de-motivating, unless you have a high conversion rate.

Finally, you need to know the rate of commission – both the bottom line and the structure. Some businesses operate a two-tier system, where you get paid for everyone who clicks through to your affiliate, and then receive a further commission if they complete a purchase. Other businesses just pay for one or the other. Commission rates for affiliates vary considerably from less than one percent for clicks to as much as 75% for some digital download products.

However, it's more realistic to work on a figure between 5% and 20%, and it's worth comparing similar companies to see if their commission rates and terms and conditions are similar.

Remember that money is important no doubt but you will also have to consider several other factors that will help you judge whether the products and services offered to comply with your standards. You cannot simply give anybody a nod and must lay down some ground rules for them. This might seem like a wrong thing to do but you need to maintain the standard of your blog and website as well. For this, you can send them a mail, listing the things that you will not be okay with on your blog or site such as sexually explicit content, weapons, adult products etc. There can be companies who will be looking for people that will be interested in letting out some space for such items. If they suspect that you have not explicitly mentioned these terms then they might start supplying you with links to such products. So it is important for you to try and check everything that they send across just to be cautious.

You must also discuss the rights and obligations and agree upon a termination clause. Remember, if you follow a path that is extremely professional, then it will be easy for you. You cannot take anything too lightly or casually, especially during the initial stages. Make sure you have everything signed and attested just to maintain an official record of your alliance and agreement. Once you are satisfied with everything and have made up your mind to go ahead with the deal then there should be nothing in your way to stop you.

Avoid paid-for programs

When you type 'Affiliate Marketing Programs' into Google, you will be inundated with hits. Some of these will be companies who ask you to pay to join their program. They will make use of fancy pamphlets that you can download and mention a well thought out payment plan. What's more, they will probably offer you a huge 'discount' to climb on board. The program's normal sign up cost is $99, but for today only, you will be admitted for the special price of just $20 – it may even be less than that. They will, in fact, make it look extremely attractive by canceling out the $99 with a big red cross and write $20 only next to it. All you have to do now is close the window and move away from such programs.

It goes without saying that there are a million suspicious websites out there all of whom promise you something but do something else. Now, while I am not saying that these people might cheat you, even if they are to charge you a high amount of money it will be for their profit and they will not be bothered about you or your website. So don't trust these and only trust your instincts in doing the right thing.

As has already been noted, the affiliate business doesn't pay any commission to you until they make a sale and remember this is a sale they wouldn't ace without your help. So why would they want you to pay for the privilege of widening their retail reach? It was mentioned before that nobody would be willing to part with their money just to promote someone else. That's like saying Microsoft wants to hire you but you need to pay them fees for it.

It can sometimes feel like the right choice to make, especially if the website you visited is promising you many things. I am sure you have also considered it many times just to get started with affiliate marketing at the earliest. You have to be more patient when it comes to affiliate marketing because, otherwise, you might end up getting scammed.

But who in their right senses would use their credit card details or check into their online banking account to transfer money to a suspicious source? Not only is it dangerous for your account but what if you end up having an identity theft?

So, as a rule of thumb, don't trust any website on affiliate marketing that promises you good business if you pay them some money first. That is not how it works and you will have to find a different way in order for you to establish a proper affiliate marketing set up.

Remember, if you stay too long on a website you will be tempted to check it out in detail. Instead, choose to exit as soon as possible and also clear your cookies.

Another thing that seems to happen is that companies charge affiliates to join deals in high-ticket items. You may make a tasty profit from each conversion, but realistically are the people who will be visiting your site going to be interested in high-ticket stuff, even if it is linked to your niche? Even if you can answer 'yes' to that one, you're a beginner in the affiliate marketing game. Isn't it better to make your mistakes for free?

Check the Business

We've established that any affiliate you pair with should complement and add value to your site for your visitors, as well as return an income for you. We read on how it is possible for you to increase the number of customers that visit the affiliates page and how much more business both of you can establish together if you understand each other well.

But in order for this to happen, you must initiate the process of looking for the best affiliates to tie up with. So make sure that you do some research and try and choose the best one. After all, you have the choice to nod or refuse a certain client depending on whether or not you like them.

One way to look for the good ones is by checking out what other blogs like yours are hosting. You can randomly check the websites that other bloggers like you are hosting, especially the popular ones. Once you have a few, you can decide to contact them yourself and show them your blog or website. After you get a reply, you can skim through all the important ones.

Maybe you've looked at a few business websites and are wondering who to approach. You can decide to shortlist 5 or 6 of them and go to the next step.

The first thing to do is check out the website for navigation. Is it easy to find the products your visitors will be interested in, and how easy is it to complete the purchase once the affiliate link takes the reader to the product?

This is important because you have to believe in the website yourself before you decide to host them for others. You will have to place yourself in the shoes of others just so that you have a chance to look at your blog from a third party perspective. For this, you must understand how the affiliate website operates.

One way to check this out is to place an order on the site yourself, so you can check out the purchase process on behalf of your visitors. Is the navigation process straightforward, from adding the item to your virtual basket? Is it possible for you to edit the items present in your cart? Can you increase or decrease the volume of the products easily? Does it have an option to add in a coupon code? Is it possible to redeem any points? What about the payment process? Does the site support PayPal?

Many online purchasers are wary about using credit cards online and prefer the speed, simplicity, and security of paying via PayPal. And it's worth returning an item so that you can check out their standards of customer service. By placing affiliate links on your site, you are effectively endorsing the company and its products to your followers, so you need to know they will get good service.

Imagine what would happen if you start putting links to websites that are slightly tough to navigate or the buying process is complicated? People won't be interested in clicking on the links and the company might not garner as many hits as is necessary.

Once you've checked out that side of the business, and are completely satisfied with what you have, it's time to speak to someone about becoming an affiliate, so that any queries you have can be addressed before you commit yourself.

Make sure you have everything sorted out and jot down the questions in terms of importance and priority. Once sorted, start asking them one by one if it is a telephone chat or you can also shoot them a mail with all your queries. Remember, it is never a bad idea to be well informed about something. After all, you are hosting their website and it is best that they give answers to everything that you wish to know. It might take them some time to get back to you and you can give them a couple of days' time to go through all your questions and answer them one by one.

If nobody is available for you, or they keep you waiting for several days for a reply, maybe you should move on. After all, if they can't make the effort to answer your queries before you become a partner, it isn't likely that they will do so once you've joined the program. So don't keep waiting on someone who is not keen on replying to you even if they say things like "sorry for the delay, we regret it."

Chapter 6: Affiliate Marketing Via Social Media Networks

Affiliate marketing via the various social media networks is, perhaps, the most fun way, and of course, a great way to enhance earnings. Working as an affiliate allows you to straight away start earning money without the hassles associating with creating, packaging, and advertising a product on your own.

Affiliate marketing via the social media allows you to leverage on the goodwill of your friends, family, and followers to get plenty of traffic and sales which in turn will get you good money. This chapter gives you some insight on how to use your social media platforms to increase affiliate income.

Create a redirect link for the affiliate – Instead of embedding a raw link (that very few people will be interesting in clicking) on your FB page, create and insert a redirect link that will take the visitor to the advertiser's site.

Quality content – As in the case of your blog, here too, create quality content first. This will attract more visitors to your page and the increased traffic can then be rerouted to affiliate links. A compelling story fitted with a link at the end is a sure shot winner. The content you create could take any form: a blog post, an FB post, YouTube video, a Podcast, and more.

Ensure you have images of the product(s) that you are promoting – A visual treat is always better remembered and retained by the human brain than mere text even if the text is highly compelling. Ensure you have a picture or a link to the picture of the product to enhance chances of the sale closing successfully.

53

Create and grow you email list from your social media connections – One critical aspect to note here is that social media sites themselves work as affiliates and hence if you aggressively use that platform to grow your affiliate income, you could be banned. While keeping this in mind, you could create and grow an email list from your social media contacts and connections and then send your affiliate links through email. This will help you mitigate the "banning" risk while giving you headway into genuinely interested buyers of the products and services you are promoting.

Promote only genuine and good-quality offers – Be wary of fraud and cheap offers and promote the really good ones only. This attitude makes you and your social connections happy; you will be happy that you are getting paid well by way of healthy commissions and your friends will be happy that they have access to a great deal.

Leverage the power of autoresponder emails – Autoresponder tools such as Aweber are powerful inventions that are extremely handy for affiliates. You could set the responder to send 7 emails (one every day for the first 7 days) after a new person connects with you. These emails can be any value-addition mails such as e-courses and study materials that are relevant for the subscriber. This value-addition offering will make the person your fan for life and he or she will be more inclined to click on affiliate links that you send to them or embed on your social media page.

The above strategies are great ways to increase your fan base on social media and then leverage that large base to generate sales and leads under your affiliate marketing program. Social media reaches every nook and corner of the world and it would be foolhardy not to take advantage of this huge reach and dig into untapped business opportunities.

Chapter 7: Affiliate Marketing Scams

As a novice in the highly challenging field of affiliate marketing, it is extremely important for you not to fall for scams and fraudulent networks and advertisers. The field of affiliate marketing per se is very legitimate but like any other industry, it is prone to misuse by mischief mongers and scamsters looking for a quick buck. Here are some of the common scams that you are bound to come across as you learn the ropes of the affiliate marketing.

Fraudulent Training Programs – Like all newbies in any field, wanting to attend a course is a common thing you would like to do before you plunge into the game. There will be hundreds of entities promising you the world and telling you that they have a magic wand to make you rich overnight with affiliate marketing.

Do not fall for such cheap gimmicks. Most likely, they are people waiting to make a fast buck by giving you material that has little or no real substance. You will merely lose out on the fees that you paid to join the course. Check, find out more, ask people who have done the course before, and only then make the fee payment and complete the training.

Get Rich Overnight Offers – There are hundreds of fraudulent mails floating around that promise you anything between $2000 and $10000 within a week by working for just 2-3 hours a day. Again, beware of such marketing gimmicks. You know it cannot be true. If it was true, there would be a huge line of aspirants and this kind of project (if true) would never need a marketing strategy. It would sell by itself. On the contrary, such "too good to be true" scenarios would ideally be kept secret.

There is no such thing in a legitimate affiliate marketing program. It entails all the hard work and diligence already spelt out in this book and nothing less to make a success of the program and make a decent amount of money regularly.

No Service or Product to sell – These offers are completely fraudulently. If someone is willing to shell out money without wanting anything in return, you should know that it is a straightforward fraud. These seeming "business opportunities" are structured like a pyramid where money is simply passed on and there is no one actually making any money. You will not only lose your investment but also please know that such schemes are totally illegal.

Programs that need you to make an initial payment – All legitimate affiliate programs are completely free. If someone is asking for initial payment, then your antennae should go up and you should totally avoid that person and/or email.

Scams based on Domain names – Here too there are multiple emails floating around that tell you the following story: The fraudsters can see from some unnamed or fancily named records that xyz.com is registered in your name and someone else in the country of origin of this scam (usually China) wants to register his or her domain name as xyz.cn. To protect your business interests, they will want you to send some money and then all payments in relation to xyz.cn will also start flowing to you!

This is utter rubbish; do not fall for it. If you send that initial payment, you can say goodbye to it forever, because if you notice you never owned the domain name xyz.com at all!!

Avoid all these kinds of scams by doing due diligence. Ask

around, ask Google, look up the company website that is selling you these programs, and finally if it is too good to be true and then it is definitely not true. Do not fall for it and stay away!

Remember as long as there are people to fool, mock at and cheat, there will be people fooling, mocking and making a quick buck by cheating! Do not be one of those who fall for these kinds of "easy" money fast and without thinking.

Chapter 8: Affiliate Marketing without a Website

One of the most common ways in which you can launch yourself into the world of affiliate marketing is by creating a website. And if you are in it for the long haul, then it will be in the best interest of your business that you create a website.

However, if you are still at the stage of learning about web designing or if you are amongst those who are not interested in creating a website, but still want to be a part of affiliate marketing, then fret not because there is an easy solution to this problem. And in this chapter, you will learn about the various ways in which you can get started with affiliate marketing without the use of a website.

Remember that the main objective of affiliate marketing is to provide you with a way in which you can put up your affiliate link in front of the target audience. As mentioned earlier, building a website is the most common approach adopted. But then again, the path you opt for is entirely up to you. With this basic objective in mind, let us look at various methods that you can use for getting your affiliate link to the target audience.

Ads and Reviews

You can use classified sites to promote your affiliate product. You must already be familiar with websites like Craigslist, eBay and so on to look for any product you want. The same can be used to promote your affiliate product too. You can write ads or even reviews about your affiliate products and then post them along with the affiliate link.

Viral Marketing

Viral marketing means spreading awareness about something very quickly. So, for doing this, you will need to figure out a product that can go viral online. A viral product is a product that has been created with the specific intention to spread it quickly to a large number of people. This is one of the fastest ways in which you can gain attention for your product.

What you can do perhaps is write a very short eBook, preferably less than 30 pages or even a report on a particular topic that interests you, and then insert the links to your affiliate products in it. Then you can distribute it to the audience using whichever means you have in mind. You could sell it, put it up on other websites or even just casually inform people that they can buy it. For starters, you can start selling this eBook on eBay for a nominal price. Ensure that whatever you are writing about is actually informational and useful. No one would want to go through a document filled with affiliate links.

Pay per Click (PPC)

This is not a method that would come as recommended. In this method, you will have to create a lot of pay per click or PPC campaigns making use of search engines like Google, Yahoo, Bing, etc. and then you will have to promote the merchant website by making use of your affiliate link. So, this is not a straightforward method because instead of directly making use of PPC to promote your own affiliate link, you will send all this to your merchant.

There are two things that you will need to know about before selecting this option. It might just happen that the merchant website might not accept your affiliate link. You will have to compete with other advertisers for the space available. And you might as well forget about your ad if it isn't well written and it is not attractive and not just this but you will even have to bid an amount higher than the rest. And the second aspect is that you will have no quality control over the merchant's page. If the merchant website does not have proper content or it is of poor quality, then you would probably end up paying a larger sum than necessary.

Blogs and Forums

All you have to do is zero in on a product that interests you and you are keen on promoting, then start marketing this product by posting about it on various forums and blogs. The question is how do you direct the users to your affiliate link? Well, the answer is quite simple because all you have to do is make use of your affiliate link as your signature. If you make yourself an active member on any forum and if you have followers, then this will just be an added advantage. But then again, you should be cautious about the kind of blogs and forums you decide to post about your products on. You need to post on such blogs and forums that deal with a topic complimentary to your own product or at least along similar lines to what you are promoting. If you want to market a fashion affiliated product, then you might not find any enthusiastic supporters on a forum meant for car parts.

Along the same line of thought, if you are really interested in making a big splash on any public forum, then you will need to be careful about the content you are posting. Ensure that the content is not only interesting but helpful too. Try becoming an active member of the forum. And once you have managed to establish yourself and garnered the attention of others, then a greater number of users will want to visit your link. And also remember to maintain some etiquette while posting online.

Don't spam the blog or forum with unnecessary posts, as this might eventually lead to you being banned from the forum or your posts might be deleted.

YouTube

YouTube is one of the most popular ways in which you can get your message across to literally millions of users within no time. YouTube has nearly a billion visitors every month. That is simply incredible and you could very well use it to your advantage. All you need is a webcam, an innovative idea and the internet. These three things are more than enough to start your own channel on YouTube. You can insert your affiliate links in the description of your channel and even in your videos. In this manner, you will be able to convert your followers into affiliate users and this will generate profits for you.

Select a niche you are interested in, and once you have decided that, then you can start a video series about it and you can insert your affiliate links into it. The viewers would already be interested in the video series created by you and, for this reason, it is likely that they would even be curious about the affiliate product you are promoting.

There are two rules and you should abide by them if you want to use this method successfully. The first rule is that the content you are posting should provide the viewers with some value and monetary gain for you should be a secondary objective. If you start the series with only the monetary aspect in your mind and want to make money from your link, then this behavior will get you listed as spam and all the hard work you put into this will be useless. If what you have produced is meaningful and interesting, then the chances of gaining attention and even respect of likely users will increase. The second rule is that you don't create something that is misleading. You would be violating YouTube's policies if the video you have posted is unrelated to the link or even if the title or description is misleading. This is something that you would want to avoid.

Video marketing on YouTube is easy, but then, if you aren't careful, it can be quite risky. It is highly likely that the affiliate links can be branded as spam. So the best way to avoid this is by being honest and being useful. Ensure that you have quality controls in place and the content is meaningful. Don't indulge in any behavior that can be listed as spam. If you are interested in nutrition then you could have instructional videos related to cooking or you could even have discussions related to this topic. Anything that might prove to be useful for the viewers is the best way to gain attention.

There are some precautions you can take to ensure that your videos aren't listed as spam. The first thing you can do is to not include too many affiliate links in your video. It is better to include one link in your description and another one in the video, provided it is relevant. The second thing you can do is to mention that the link is an affiliate link or that you are an affiliate. You can also contact YouTube to ensure that you aren't in any trouble. If you have managed to acquire a valuable viewership then this means that the chance of making money from your affiliate links will increased.

Hub

A Hub is like a miniature of a website, it is just a page. So, on this page, you can talk about anything that you are interested in. You can base your content on the affiliate market and related products you are interested in.

Your Hub would be put up on the HubPages site and it is perfectly alright even if you don't have any knowledge about web designing. You can still make it look decent and professional. The advantage of making use of Hub is that you don't have to code the page in HTML. You can create the page on any topic you are interested in. You can insert various ads, reviews or any other content that you want.

Another good feature of this is that it is even a social networking platform. Even being simply present on HubPages you can attract traffic towards the topics you are interested in.

Conclusion

Affiliate marketing is here to stay and with an intention to be a stakeholder in this rather interesting and lucrative field you should endeavor to pick up the right skills, know the correct information, and understand how to implement your learning prudently before you plunge in.

It is a great career opportunity for those who have managed to break the code and have made sustained and persistent efforts without being demoralized by initial setbacks. Making an entry into this challenging environment, getting that first small break, coding and decoding large amounts of data and information to leverage to your advantage, and most importantly a willingness to learn from your failures; all these require lots of hard work, diligence, and commitment from your side.

Yes, it is a huge challenge to overcome; but once done, the opportunities are unlimited for you. Heartened by this knowledge, I hope you pick up this chance to enhance your earnings.

And finally, do not fall for scamsters and cheats. Think before you leap; use common sense and avoid things that do not make sense. There are hundreds of legitimate ways of making money vide affiliate marketing. Although the process of setting up and maintenance may seem tough, it is quite possible to make a success of your venture.

There are many people making great amounts of money. Follow them; be motivated by them, and find the courage to start off. In fact, I believe, that affiliate marketing business opportunities if leveraged well can be a legacy to leave behind for your future generation.

Thank you again for purchasing this book!

I hope this book was able to help you to start off on the exciting and lucrative journey of affiliate marketing. The next step for you is to start implementing your learning and set up actionable tasks which should be reviewed regularly to see if you are going down the right path.

CPSIA information can be obtained
at www.ICGtesting.com
Printed in the USA
LVHW090007100221
678883LV00010B/318